What's out in Space?

Susan Mayes

Designed by Steve Page
Illustrated by Martin Newton, Chris Lyon and Joseph McEwan
Science consultant: Sue Becklake
Cover design by Russell Punter
Cover illustration by Christyan Fox
With thanks to Sarah Cronin

CONTENTS

Space watching

At night, when the sky is clear, you can see hundreds of stars far out in space. On most nights you can see the Moon as well.

If you want a better look at the Moon, you can use binoculars to make it look bigger and closer.

The Solar System

The things you can see in the sky at night only make up a little of what's out in space. Our planet, Earth, is in one tiny part of space called the Solar System.

The Solar System is made up of nine planets, lots of moons and lumps of rock called asteroids. There are also balls of ice and rock called comets. Everything moves around the Sun.

Moons move around planets. Earth has one moon, but some planets have lots.

Sun

Jupiter

Mercury

Earth

Moon

Venus

Mars

Astronomers

An astronomer is someone who looks at things in space. People have been doing this for thousands of years.

A modern astronomer uses a telescope to see things further away than you could ever imagine.

This picture shows the order of the planets from the Sun outward. They are many millions of km apart. Some are rock, like the Earth. Others are made of liquids and gases.

The Sun is the biggest thing in the Solar System. It is made of glowing, hot gases. But there is much more in space than this. Everything we know about in space is called the Universe.

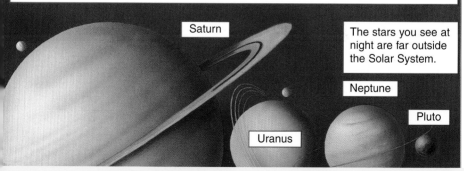

Saturn

The stars you see at night are far outside the Solar System.

Neptune

Pluto

Uranus

Internet link Go to **www.usborne-quicklinks.com** for a link to a website where you can take a virtual tour of the Solar System.

Light and dark

The Sun is the only thing in the Solar System which makes light. Nothing else has light of its own.

Astronomers can only see planets and moons because the Sun shines on them and makes them show up.

Moving around

Each planet goes around the Sun on its own invisible path called an orbit.

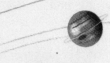

Pluto

Earth

Earth takes just over 365 days to orbit the Sun once. This time makes one Earth year.

Planets further away from the Sun than Earth take much longer to make one orbit. Pluto takes 248 Earth years.

Day and night

As the Earth makes its long journey around the Sun, it turns all the time. It makes one turn every 24 hours.

When your side of Earth faces the Sun, you have day. When you are turned away from the Sun, it is night.

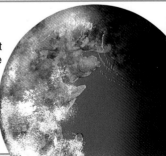

You cannot always see the Sun, but it shines in space all the time.

*Pictures with the symbol 🖙 can be downloaded from **www.usborne-quicklinks.com***

Watching the Moon

At night, the Moon seems to shine brightly, but the light you see is really from the Sun. It shines on half of the Moon all the time and lights it up.

Use binoculars to take a closer look at the Moon. The big dark patches are mainly flat areas called seas, but there is no water in them. The dark rings are craters. They were made by space rocks which crashed into the Moon.

The Moon's shape

The Moon moves around the Earth all the time. Each night you can see a different amount of the bright side. Sometimes you can see more of it and sometimes you can see less. The Moon's shape does not really change.

You cannot see a New Moon. The Sun shines on the other side.

This is a Crescent Moon. You can only see part of the side lit by the Sun.

This is a Full Moon. You can see all of the bright side lit by the Sun.

Internet link Go to **www.usborne-quicklinks.com** for a link to a website with online activities about day and night and the phases of the Moon.

Going to the Moon

The hardest part of going into space is getting off the ground. This is because of something invisible called gravity. Gravity pulls everything near the Earth back to the ground.

If you throw a ball up in the air, it comes down again. It is gravity which pulls the ball back. Without gravity, the ball would go up into space.

Breaking away

A spacecraft going to the Moon has to break away from Earth's gravity. A powerful rocket blasts it into space to escape the strong pull. The spacecraft gets to the Moon in about three days.

Gravity in space

There is gravity around planets and moons, but there is less gravity out in space.

Astronauts in space feel weightless because there is less gravity to hold them down.

The spacecraft is only the small part near the top. The other parts carry the fuel needed to power the rocket.

The Moon is the only place in space where people have landed. On 20th July 1969, American astronauts were the first people to land there. They went in the Apollo 11 spacecraft.

When the astronauts walked on the Moon, they seemed to float with each step. This is because the Moon's gravity is weaker than Earth's, so it did not pull them down so strongly.

Neil Armstrong was the first person to walk on the Moon.

The astronauts left scientific instruments on the Moon. They also collected rock and dust to take back to Earth.

The Lunar Module took the astronauts down to the Moon while Apollo 11 stayed in space.

It was very hot in the sunlight but very cold at night. The astronauts had to take their own air supply in tanks because there is no air on the Moon.

The Moon's surface is dry and dusty. There is no wind to blow the soil around or rain to wash it away. Footprints will stay there forever.

Internet links Go to www.usborne-quicklinks.com for links to websites where you can watch a video clip of the first Moon-walk and see views of the Moon's surface.

7

About the Sun

The Sun is the most important thing in the Solar System. It gives the planets their light and heat. Its gravity stops the planets from flying off into space.

The Sun is really a medium-sized star. Many stars you see at night are bigger and brighter than it is. They look small because they are so far away.

Where the Sun came from

Scientists think that the Sun and the planets may have formed inside a huge cloud of gas and dust in space.

The gas and dust were squashed together in the middle of the cloud and this part became very hot. This is where the Sun began. The planets formed at about the same time.

DANGER!

Never look directly at the Sun, or with binoculars or a telescope. The strong light will seriously damage your eyes.

What the Sun is like

The Sun is not a ball of rock like the Earth. It is made of hot glowing gases which make it look like a fiery ball. Huge amounts of light and heat come from the surface.

Giant bursts of gas are thrown up from the Sun's surface. They are called flares and prominences. They look like flames.

Hiding the Sun

Sometimes the Moon comes between the Sun and the Earth and covers up the Sun. This is an eclipse of the Sun.

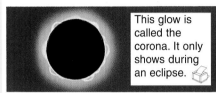

This glow is called the corona. It only shows during an eclipse.

The Moon is much smaller than the Sun but it can hide the Sun from our view. This happens because the Moon is much closer to us.

How it works

You can blot out a ceiling light by holding a coin in front of your eye. Cover the other eye with your hand.

Because the coin is close to your eye, it can easily blot out the light, which is further away. The Moon can blot out the Sun in the same way.

Life on Earth

Sunspots are darker patches. They are cooler than the rest of the surface.

Nothing would live or grow on Earth without the Sun's light and heat. The Earth's atmosphere only lets through the light and heat we need to live, keeping out the Sun's harmful rays.

Internet links Go to *www.usborne-quicklinks.com* for links to websites where you can watch an eclipse of the Sun and find lots of Sun facts.

9

Exploring the planets

Scientists can find out more about the planets by sending machines called probes out into space. These do not carry people, only special equipment.

Next to the Sun

Mercury is the closest planet to the Sun. It has mountains and craters like our Moon, but it is much hotter.

The American probe, Mariner 10, passed Mercury three times. It sent back pictures.

Our closest planet

Venus is Earth's closest planet. Its rocky surface is very hot and its air is thick and poisonous.

This Russian probe, Venera 9, sent back the first pictures from the surface.

The red planet

This is the American probe, Viking 2.

Mars is the planet which is most like Earth. It has mountains, valleys and volcanoes, but it has a pink sky. Mars is covered with red dust.

Going further

It takes a probe many years to reach planets far away from the Sun.

The American probes, Pioneers 10 and 11, have been to the edge of the Solar System, exploring planets on the way.

Internet links Go to www.usborne-quicklinks.com for links to websites where you can see animated timelines of space probes and find out about their discoveries.

The giants

Jupiter and Saturn are the biggest planets in the Solar System. They are made of gases and liquids. The American probes Voyager 2 and Pioneer 11 have been to take a look at them. Pioneer 10 also went to look at Jupiter.

Saturn has many thin rings made up of small pieces of ice. They form bright bands.

Jupiter is the largest of all the planets. It has a patch called the Great Red Spot. This is a huge long-lasting storm.

Voyager 2

The green planet

Uranus is a gas planet like Jupiter and Saturn. It is the only planet which spins on its side.

Voyager's last visit

The probe, Voyager 2, was sent into space in 1977. It had to travel for 12 years before it reached the planet Neptune.

The smallest planet

Pluto is the smallest planet in the Solar System. It is dark and icy. Its moon, Charon, is about half its size.

Voyager 2 did not visit Pluto, so there is still a lot to find out.

Neptune has a large, dark spot. This may be a storm, like Jupiter's Great Red Spot. There is a smaller spot as well.

Neptune's biggest moon, Triton, is cold and icy. It is reddish-pink.

Voyager found six new moons and three faint rings. The rings can only be seen with special instruments.

Scientists call this cloud the scooter because it speeds around Neptune faster than the other clouds.

Voyager 2 left Neptune and moved out of the Solar System. It will keep going out into space, even when all its machines stop working.

Internet link Go to **www.usborne-quicklinks.com** for a link to a website where you can watch a video of Voyager's incredible journey.

Visitors from space

Comets are balls of ice and rock which move in huge orbits around the Sun. A comet sometimes comes into our part of the Solar System from beyond Pluto.

Halley's Comet comes back every 76 years.

The hard icy middle of the comet is called a nucleus. When the comet gets near the Sun, the ice boils away and makes a tail of gas and dust.

Asteroids

Between Mars and Jupiter there are thousands of rocks called asteroids. They orbit the Sun in a ring called the asteroid belt. Some asteroids are hundreds of miles across.

Meteors

Sometimes a space rock or a speck of dust speeds into the Earth's air. It burns up making a streak of light called a meteor or a shooting star. You can sometimes see one at night.

Making craters

Big space rocks which crash into planets or moons are called meteorites. Most of our Moon's craters were made by meteorites billions of years ago.

This crater is in Arizona, America.

There used to be craters on Earth, but they have been worn away over thousands of years. The crater in this picture is over 1 km (0.6 mile) across.

Looking at stars

If you could count all the stars you see in the night sky, there would be over a thousand. Astronomers can see millions more with telescopes.

What a star is

A star is a ball of glowing gases just like the Sun, our closest star. Light from nearly all stars takes thousands of years to reach us on Earth.

Most stars move around each other in groups of two or more. From Earth these groups usually look like a single star. Our Sun is unusual because it is on its own.

Why stars twinkle

Starlight has to pass through the Earth's air before it reaches us. The air moves and changes all the time. It makes a star's light look brighter, then dimmer, so it seems to twinkle.

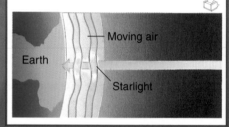

Moving air

Earth

Starlight

Galaxies

Stars belong to spinning groups called galaxies. There are millions of galaxies and each one has millions of stars. Our Solar System is in a spiral-shaped galaxy called the Milky Way.

Internet link Go to *www.usborne-quicklinks.com* for a link to a website where you can watch a short movie about the life cycle of stars.

The life of a star

A star begins in a gas cloud called a nebula. The cloud collapses and squashes together. Its middle gets so hot that it glows as a new star.

The star shines brightly for many millions of years, then it swells up and becomes much cooler. This huge star is called a red giant.

The outer layers of the red giant disappear into space. A piece called a core is left behind. It shrinks to a small star called a white dwarf.

Exploding stars

Some big, heavy stars grow into enormous supergiant stars which can explode into space. An exploding star is called a supernova.

Black holes

When some stars explode they leave a big core. It shrinks and becomes small but very heavy. Its strong gravity sucks everything in, even light. It is called a black hole.

Space shuttles

The Americans have built a kind of spacecraft called a space shuttle. The first American shuttle flew in 1981. A shuttle is a launch vehicle that blasts into space like a rocket, but it comes back to land on a runway like a glider. It can travel into space again and again.

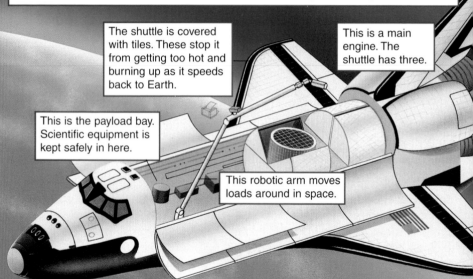

The shuttle is covered with tiles. These stop it from getting too hot and burning up as it speeds back to Earth.

This is a main engine. The shuttle has three.

This is the payload bay. Scientific equipment is kept safely in here.

This robotic arm moves loads around in space.

Inside the American shuttle the astronauts can launch machines called satellites into space from the payload bay.

On some flights, a special room called Spacelab is put inside the payload bay. Scientists do all kinds of experiments in here.

Internet link Go to **www.usborne-quicklinks.com** for a link to a website where you can watch a shuttle launch and find out more about space shuttles.

The "flying armchair"

Sometimes, astronauts leave the shuttle to work out in space. They are often strapped into a machine known as the "flying armchair".

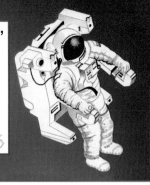

This "flying armchair" is pushing the astronaut closer to a satellite. The astronaut is steering using hand controls.

Space journey

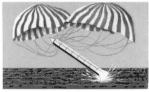

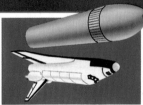

The shuttle is blasted into space by its own engines and two large booster rockets.

The rockets parachute into the sea when their fuel is used up. They will be used again.

When the shuttle has used all the fuel in the huge tank, the tank falls away.

In orbit, the payload bay doors open. The astronauts begin to work and do experiments.

When the shuttle comes back to Earth it gets red hot because it is going so fast.

The shuttle does not use engines to land. It glides down onto a long runway.

About satellites

A satellite is a thing which moves around something bigger than itself in space. There are natural satellites such as moons. They orbit planets.

The satellites on these pages are machines. They are launched into orbit by a rocket or space shuttle. They carry equipment to do their work.

High above the world

Different kinds of satellites are put into different orbits. Some move in high orbits, around the middle of the Earth. They move in time with Earth so they stay above the same place.

Television satellites orbit the Earth. So do other kinds.

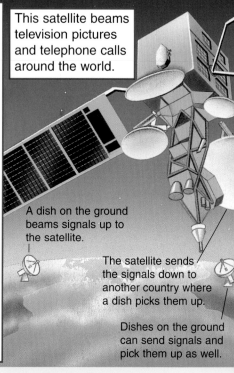

This satellite beams television pictures and telephone calls around the world.

Satellites watching Earth, orbit like this. So do some weather satellites.

Other satellites make low orbits over the top of the Earth. They go around it several times a day. The Earth turns below them, so they pass over a different part on each orbit.

A dish on the ground beams signals up to the satellite.

The satellite sends the signals down to another country where a dish picks them up.

Dishes on the ground can send signals and pick them up as well.

*Internet link Go to **www.usborne-quicklinks.com** for a link to a website where you can build a satellite online and find out lots more about satellites.*

The small squares on the panels are solar cells. They change sunlight into electricity to power the satellite.

There are hundreds of satellites orbiting the Earth. In the night sky they look like slowly moving stars.

Small satellite dishes on many houses pick up television signals.

Watching the weather

This satellite takes pictures of clouds moving around the Earth and measures the temperature of the air.

The information is beamed down to Earth. Scientists use it to work out what the weather may be like.

Watching space

This astronomy satellite looks out into space. It can see things that scientists cannot see from Earth.

The information from satellites can help scientists find out about things such as black holes or galaxies.

Space stations

A space station is a kind of satellite. It is big enough for people to live and work inside. Astronauts travel to the station once it is in orbit.

The first space stations

America and Russia have both launched space stations. The Russians sent up their first Salyut station in 1971. The Americans launched Skylab in 1973.

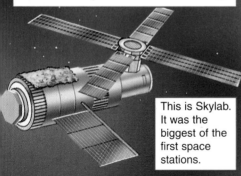

This is Skylab. It was the biggest of the first space stations.

The space stations were launched using rockets. Astronauts visited them for a few weeks at a time and sometimes worked outside in space.

Living in space

Astronauts have to learn new ways to do ordinary things like washing and eating. These are more difficult to do in space as everything floats around.

This special shower is in a bag. It stops water drops from floating about.

Most space food is dried. Astronauts have to add water before they eat it.

Astronauts can sleep any way up in space. They don't float around because they are strapped into sleeping bags.

Internet link Go to **www.usborne-quicklinks.com** for a link to a website packed with games and fascinating facts about living in space.

Staying in Mir

In 1986 the Russians launched a space station called Mir, which stayed in space for 15 years. Extra parts called modules were added. In March 2001, Mir was brought back to Earth, and landed in the sea.

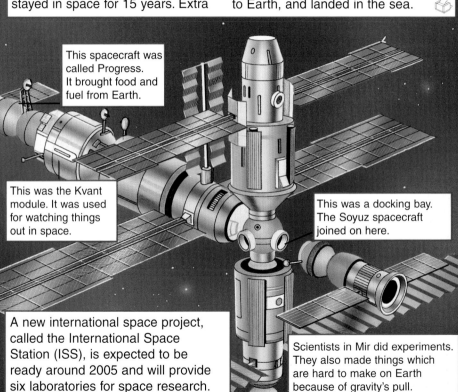

This spacecraft was called Progress. It brought food and fuel from Earth.

This was the Kvant module. It was used for watching things out in space.

This was a docking bay. The Soyuz spacecraft joined on here.

A new international space project, called the International Space Station (ISS), is expected to be ready around 2005 and will provide six laboratories for space research.

Scientists in Mir did experiments. They also made things which are hard to make on Earth because of gravity's pull.

The future in space

Scientists have made many amazing discoveries in space. Now they are making new plans and inventing new machines to help them learn more.

Telescope in space

The Hubble Space Telescope orbits high above Earth. It sees much further into space than astronomers can from the ground. It may discover far off planets with signs of life on them.

More about probes

Probes have been sent to Jupiter and Saturn. One called Galileo has orbited Jupiter. Another, called Cassini, is going to orbit Saturn.

Galileo has sent a smaller probe down into Jupiter's clouds.

The probes can also visit some of the moons circling the planets. They can send pictures and information back to Earth over several years.

Space planes

There may soon be a plane which can fly into space and then speed to anywhere on Earth in an hour.

Space planes would also be able to carry satellites out into space and visit space stations.